Typeset in Garamond Regular
Manufactured in the United Kingdom

A Night Before Christmas
The Alternative Tale

Alex Hales

Illustrated by Stew Wright

'T was the night before Christmas, round the back of the sleigh

and a worse-for-wear reindeer had been drinking all day;

when Santa and the gang were depending on him,

well, bollocks to them! He'd been at the gin...

The mulled wine, the sherry, liqueur cherries too,
with overtime aplenty, what was a reindeer to do?
His name was Rudy and the part he would play
was lost as he lazed half passed out in the hay,

4

Rudy slumped amongst presents and questioned his fate;

Santa cursed that *that moose* had forgotten the date.

Santa swore as he searched until lo and behold…

a chainsaw of snoring, a red gleam in the cold!

But, how could he be napping oan this night ay the year?

When Santa got his hands on him, he'd kick him into gear;

and so he shook Rudy out of his deep and peaceful sleep,

propped him straight and waited... but he flopped again in a heap.

'Ah'll wring yer antlers,' Santa said. 'That's what ah'm gonnae do.'

To which a befuddled deer replied, 'just who the fuck are you?'

'Red suit, chubby belly, doesnae the beard ring a bell?'

But Rudy only hiccupped and thus the penny fell.

Said Santa, '*please dinnae tell me ye've goatten steaming drunk?*'
So Rudy tried to play right down the alcohol he'd sunk;
'*But ye wi' yer schnoz so bright, who will guide us now?*'
'I think that I will be just fine.' And Rudy took a bow.

'Oh ma sleighs,' said Santa. '*Oaf yer reindeer tits again,*
ye tell me ye've hud one or two when really ye've hud ten;
the kids wouldnae thank ye.' Santa's hands were on his hips.
'Jolly old elf? You're just a wan –' But Rudy's stomach flipped.

Santa strapped him up the front, amongst Dasher, Dancer, Donner:

'Fall asleep ye red-nosed runt an' know that yer a gonner;

ye always were a problem deer –' 'But Santa, I'm seeing twos!'

'Double trouble then, when we get back, will hardly sound like news.'

Comet gave to Rudy coffee to sober him up quick,

but had to hold back his antlers when he started to be sick.

Santa clicked his fingers, whistled to all a swift depart,

but Rudy raised a reindeer revolution from the heart:

'We're overworked and underpaid and freezing off our balls.'
Said Santa, '*ye keep talking 'cause the cans ay mutt food call!*'
Rudy propositioned Vixen: 'do you like my jingle bells?'
Earned himself a kick from Cupid and then his whole face swelled;

It was a red-nosed, black-eyed reindeer that led their starry way,

seeing triple chimney tops, a rear-view spinning sleigh.

'*Ye've let doon weans everywhere,*' Santa reminded him,

on the roof of the first house before Prancer pushed Rudy in.

Rudy clattered to the hearthrug, with Santa stuck behind,

who said – '*sit still, thir's stockings tae fill* –' but what should Rudy find...

only a carrot, a mince pie, a glistening glass of whiskey;

with *nothing* like hair-of-the-dog, he downed it really swiftly:

24

'This present delivering malarkey's way better when you're pissed;'
he slurred, 'I love you Santa,' and under the mistletoe they kissed.
'G'off me, ye drunken furball! Thir's places we need tae be.'
Rudy said, 'I'm sorry, old bean, but I think I need a wee.'

W ith an unzip of the flies, he whipped out his reindeer rodger;

Santa rolled his eyes and Rudy said, 'you daft old todger –

after your mulled cider sesh, the one to judge is *so* not you,'

but then a squawk of farts escaped before Rudy followed through.

Said Santa, '*fuck a duck in a pear tree; Ah hear someone, run!*'

Rudy reached out for a stocking in order to wipe his bum.

He clambered back up to the roof with it still hung from one cheek,

and as he shuffled from foot to foot said, 'I need another leak.'

'*W*hat have I said about *shitting inside?*' sang out into the fog –
curses smoked from the chimney; Rudy feared for the family's dog.
Santa strapped him on the sleigh now, under a blanket out of sight
and only his glowy nose poked into the remnants of the night.

So not another peep was heard 'til they'd finished all their rounds;
as Santa carried Rudy in, he didn't make a sound.

Santa tucked him up warm and snuggly with a bucket by his bed,
to dream of sprouts and bubbly when he'd have a hangover instead.

Rudy muttered in his slumber what sounded like 'kebab;'
Santa growled, *'an' then ye'll chunder an' ah'm no clearing that,'*
but he chuckled in his belly as he turned out the light,
whispered, *'Merry Christmas, all, c'ept this reindeer piece ay shite.'*

Printed in Great Britain
by Amazon